Mother Love

Mother Love

A Beautiful Tribute to Motherhood

♔ Hallmark Editions

Editorial Direction: Tina Hacker
Illustrated by Noreen Bonker

The publisher wishes to thank those who have given their kind permission to reprint material included in this book. Every effort has been made to give proper acknowledgments. Any omissions or errors are deeply regretted, and the publisher, upon notification, will be pleased to make necessary corrections in subsequent editions.

Acknowledgments: "Everyday Madonna" by Richard Armour. Reprinted by permission of the author. "Young Mother" by Kay Wissinger. Reprinted by permission of *The Chicago Tribune.* "My Mother's Eyes" by Meredith Gray. From Meredith Gray's volume *Poems to Mother.* © 1937 by Crescendo Publishing Co., Boston. Reprinted by permission. "The Mother in the House" from *Ladders Through the Blue* by Hermann Hagedorn. Copyright 1925 by Doubleday & Company, Inc. Reprinted by permission of the publisher. "A Mother's Prayer" from *Shining Rain* by Helen Welshimer. Copyright 1943 by Helen Welshimer. Renewal copyright © 1971 by Ralph Welshimer. Reprinted by permission of the publishers, E. P. Dutton & Co., Inc. "The Way of a Mother" by Katherine Edelman. © 1954 by Katherine Edelman. Reprinted by permission. "What Mother Is to Me" by J. Harold Gwynne, "Like a Mother's Voice" by Homer C. Fisher and "A Mother" by Sarah N. Latham from *In Praise of Mothers,* compiled by J. Harold Gwynne. © 1947 by J. Harold Gwynne. Reprinted with permission. Excerpt from p. 443 ("There is no...someone she loves.") in *The Web and the Rock* by Thomas Wolfe. (Harper & Row, 1939.) By permission of Harper & Row, Publishers, Inc. (4th stanza) "Mothers" in *Songs of Faith* by Grace Noll Crowell. Copyright, 1939 by Harper & Row, Publishers, Inc. By permission of Harper & Row, Publishers, Inc. "A Mother's Creed" by Ozora Davis from *The Treasure Chest.* © 1965 by Charles L. Wallis. Reprinted by permission of Harper & Row, Publishers, Inc. "My Mother" by John Robert Quinn from *Words of Life.* © 1966 by Charles L. Wallis. Reprinted by permission of Harper & Row, Publishers, Inc. "Every mother has the breathtaking privilege..." by James Keller. Reprinted with permission of the author. "Corsage" by Ethel Jacobson. Reprinted by permission of the author and The Curtis Publishing Company. "Defeat" by Barbara A. Jones. Reprinted by permission of the author. Excerpt from *The Art of Living* by André Maurois. Reprinted by permission of Gerald Maurois, Executor of the Estate of André Maurois. "Land and Love" by Gladys McKee from Ave Maria. Reprinted by permission of the author. Proverbs 31:25-28 from the *Revised Standard Version Bible.* Reprinted by permission of the National Council of the Churches of Christ. "The Perfect Mother" from *The Exile* by Pearl Buck. Reprinted by permission of Harold Ober Associates Incorporated. Copyright 1936 by Pearl S. Buck. Copyright renewed. "A Mother's Birthday" reprinted by permission of Charles Scribner's Sons from *Chosen Poems* by Henry van Dyke. Copyright 1911 Charles Scribner's Sons.

© 1975, Hallmark Cards, Inc., Kansas City, Missouri. Printed in the United States of America.
Library of Congress Catalog Card Number: 74-83758. Standard Book Number: 87529-406-5.

WELCOME TO *MOTHER LOVE*

"Mother"—no word on earth can evoke more beautiful thoughts or more affectionate feelings. She is our first experience of tenderness, our earliest wisdom. Hers are the patience and kindness we grow on, the faith and inspiration we live by—the warmth and devotion we treasure through the years. Put them all together and they spell love.

Mother Love is a joyful celebration of the miracle of motherhood by writers of yesterday and today. Each page of this exquisitely designed keepsake edition pays tribute to that most remarkable woman in our lives and to the priceless gifts that she alone can bring.

Here is a book for mother that the whole family can share—a truly delightful assortment of reminiscences and reflections to warm the heart and stir the memory. For here is a lasting reminder of the many wonderful reasons why "mother" is a very special word for love.

1

To all things beautiful, God has given a crowning touch —
For the rose, there is dew…
For the candle, there is flame…
For the tree, there is autumn…
For the evening, there is moonlight…
And for mankind, there is mother love.

Herbert Farnham

FLOWERS FOR MOTHER

These velvet roses with their golden hue,
    Do they recall my very first bouquet:
    That ragged bunch of wilted dandelions
    I proudly brought one summer day to you?

The broken stems, the accidental weeds
    I brought when I was small, received the care
Of lavish blooms in later years. It's true
A mother's love is all a flower needs.

Georgia Sykes Sullivan

BLESS MOTHERS EVERYWHERE

Bless mothers everywhere
For being kind and sweet,
For teaching little hands to pray,
For guiding little feet;
Bless them for their patience
And understanding ways;
Bless them for their laughter
And tender words of praise;
Bless them for the love they give
That's constant, warm and true;
Bless them now and always
In everything they do.

Katherine Plumb

Little deeds of kindness,
    little words of love
Help to make earth happy,
    like the heaven above.

Julia A. Fletcher Carney

TO MOTHER

I hope that soon, dear mother,
    You and I may be
In the quiet room my fancy
    Has so often made for thee;

The pleasant, sunny chamber,
    The cushioned easy chair,
The book laid for your reading,
    The vase of flowers fair;

The desk beside the window
    Where the sun shines warm and bright;
And there in ease and quiet,
    The promised book you write;

While I sit close beside you,
    Content at last to see
That you can rest, dear mother,
    And I can cherish thee.

Louisa May Alcott

THE LITTLE THINGS

It is the little things that count
And give a mother pleasure—
The things her children bring to her
Which they so richly treasure…
The picture that is smudged a bit
With tiny fingerprints,
The colored rock, the lightning bugs,
The sticky peppermints,
The ragged, bright bouquet of flowers
A child brings, roots and all—
These things delight a mother's heart
Although they seem quite small.
A mother can see beauty
In the very smallest thing,
For there's a little bit of heaven
In a small child's offering.

Theresa Ann Hunt

LORD, GRANT ME WISDOM

Lord, grant me the understanding
that I might discipline my children
for their failings;
the patience that I might forgive them
their little transgressions;
the willingness to praise them
when they do something well;
and, Lord, grant me the wisdom to know
what is best for them always!

Katherine Nelson Davis

WHAT RULES THE WORLD

They say that man is mighty,
He governs land and sea,
He wields a mighty scepter
O'er lesser powers than he;

But mightier power and stronger
Man from his throne has hurled,
For the hand that rocks the cradle
Is the hand that rules the world.

William Ross Wallace

MOTHER'S BOY

Make rowdy music, little one!
Make rowdy mirth and song!
It is for life like this, my own,
That I have watched you long.

Romp in your merry ways apart,
And shout in freedom wild;
But creep at nighttime to my heart,
A tired little child.

Cora A. Watson

"Mother"
and "Love"
differ only in name,
For the miracles they work
are one and the same.

Karl Lawrence

8

A TREAT FOR MOTHER

On special days, the children
Always convince one another
That breakfast in bed is the perfect gift
For them to present to Mother.

So, on Mother's Day or my birthday,
I dutifully stay in bed,
And it isn't long till I hastily pull
The covers up over my head.

There's a crash, a hush, a soft giggle,
Then whispers outside in the hall
Before they march in with the laden tray,
Eggs, bacon, coffee and all.

And they know I'm delighted with everything
From the rose in the vase to burnt toast,
But oh, they don't know just seeing their joy
Is the present that pleases me most.

Mary Rita Hurley

MOTHERS

I think God took the fragrance of a flower,
A pure white flower, which blooms not for world praise,
But which makes sweet and beautiful some bower;
The compassion of the dew, which gently lays
Reviving freshness on the fainting earth
And gives to all the tired things new birth;
The steadfastness and radiance of stars,
Which lift the soul above confining bars;
The gladness of fair dawns; the sunset's peace;
Contentment which from "trivial rounds" asks no release;
The life which finds its greatest joy
        in deeds of love for others —
I think God took these precious things
        and made of them — Mothers.

Author Unknown

…the seeds of virtue are divine…
yet they are planted by a mother's hand
and nourished by her love.

John Grey

AT SINGING TIME

I have a little daughter
  Who's scarcely half-past three,
And in the twilight hour,
  She climbs upon my knee
And snuggles down within my arm
  With "Mother, sing to me!"

I sing about the squirrels
  That frolic in the wood,
About two furry kittens —
  One naughty and one good,
And then some tender lullabies —
  Just as a mother should.

The light grows faint, and fainter;
  The sandman guards the door;
My baby's boat drifts slowly
  Upon the slumber shore —
But if the singing stops, she cries,
  "O Mother, sing some more!"

I'm sure no prima donna,
  Adored from East to West,
Feels half the satisfaction,
  Or is so truly blest
As I, when singing to my child
  Held closely to my breast.

Not all the fame and glory
  Of divas can compare
With that deep thrill of pleasure
  Which is my humble share,
For precious are the laurel wreaths
  That singing mothers wear!

Anne P. L. Field

A MOTHER'S LOVE

A mother's love is love expressed
  In the things of every day —
  In lunches packed and laundry stacked,
  In troubles kissed away,
  In mittens found and cowlicks "downed,"
  In always being handy,
  In just-baked sweets and extra treats
  Like ice-cream cones and candy,
  In laces tied and faces dried,
  In praising grade-school art,
  In putting back together
  Every dream that falls apart,
  In all the things that demonstrate
  In one way or another
  That love is just another name
  For someone known as "Mother"!

Chris FitzGerald

It takes a hundred men to build an encampment,
      but it takes one woman to build a home.

Chinese Proverb

10

MOTHER'S RECIPES

Most women have a pantry filled
   With spices, herbs and stuff;
   Salt and sugar, yeast and flour
   But that's not quite enough.
   My Mom's the finest cook on earth
   And she told me long ago
   That bread's no good unless you add
   Some loving to the dough.
"And when you're baking pies," says she,
"A pinch of faith and trust,
   If added to the shortening makes
   A tender, flaky crust;
   And compassion by the spoonful
   In the batter of a cake
   Makes it come out light and fluffy;
   Just the finest you can make."
   Now these things can't be purchased
   In the store across the way;
   But Mother keeps them in her heart
   And uses them each day.

Reginald Holmes

CHILDREN DO NOT REALIZE

Children do not realize
How deep is mother love, how wise —
They do not fully understand
The goodness of her guiding hand,
And yet she's always held above
The childhood things that children love,

12

And as they grow the long years through,
That love for her keeps growing, too,
Until they learn the full extent
Of what a mother's love has meant,
The heartaches she's concealed within,
How truly wonderful she's been!

Author Unknown

EARTH'S GREATEST CHARMS

God made the streams that gurgle down the purple mountainside;
He made the gorgeous coloring with which the sunset's dyed.
He made the hills and covered them with glory, and He made
The sparkle on the dewdrops and the flecks of light and shade.
Then, knowing all earth needed was a climax for her charms,
He made a little woman with a baby in her arms.

He made the arching rainbow that is thrown across the sky;
He made the blessed flowers that nod and smile as we go by.
He made the gladsome beauty as she bows with queenly grace,
But, sweetest of them all, He made the love-light in the face
That bends above a baby, warding off the world's alarms —
That dainty little woman with her baby in her arms.

A soft pink wrap embellished with a vine in silken thread,
A filmy snow-white cap upon a downy little head,
A dress, 'twould make the winter drift look dusty by its side,
Two cheeks, with pure rose petal tint, two blue eyes wonder-wide,
And, bending o'er, the mother face embued with heaven's own charms —
God bless the little woman with her baby in her arms!

Author Unknown

LAND AND LOVE

Men love the land! I know they speak
Of wide green fields, of silver creek.
They think of these as set apart
Until the miles outwit the heart.

And set against the mind's bright screen
Of intimate roads and hills between
The memory and time and space…
Always a well-beloved face.

The land will narrow two by four
To lilacs shoving in the door
And softly as far church bells ringing…
A woman sweeping, dusting, singing.

Gladys McKee

When you educate a man, you educate an individual.
When you educate a woman, you educate a whole family.

Chinese Proverb

A MOTHER IS LOVE

This is a mother —
Warmth and tenderness
And soft dresses
That smell of sunshine.
Songs and stories
And smiling eyes
That say, "I love you."
Gentle hands
That can comfort a kitten,
Or shape a sugar cookie,
Or lift a little one
Close, close, close to her heart
To a lovely world
Of trust and security.
A mother personifies
Shared understanding —
Confident faith —
Unalterable love.
This is a mother.

Doris Chalma Brock

O MAGICAL WORD

O magical word, may it never die from the lips
     that love to speak it,
Nor melt away from the trusting hearts
     that even would break to keep it.
Was there ever a name that lived like thine?
     Will there ever be another?
The angels have reared in heaven a shrine
     to the holy name of Mother.

Author Unknown

A MOTHER'S WORLD

A mother's world is a gentle world:
     a world of satin and sachet…
     of hugs and kisses
     and lullabies
        as soft as moonlight…

A mother's world is a busy world:
     a world of half-price sales and shopping carts…
     of school supplies and permanent press
     and learning math
        while cooking supper…

A mother's world is a happy world:
     a world of laughter and song…
     of family fun around the dinner table
     and love that reaches out
        and lasts forever.

Barbara Burrow

TO MY MOTHER

They tell us of an Indian tree
     Which, howsoe'er the sun and sky
May tempt its boughs to wander free,
     And shoot and blossom, wide and high,
Far better loves to bend its arms
     Downward again to that dear earth
From which the life that fills and warms
     Its grateful being first had birth.
'Tis thus, though wooed by flattering friends,
     And fed with fame (if fame it may be),
This heart, my own dear mother, bends,
     With love's true instinct, back to thee!

Thomas Moore

FLOWERS FOR MOTHER

I never have a special day
To give flowers to my mother;
I give them to her every day
To show how much I love her.

When I sweep the kitchen floor,
Or care for baby brother,
Run on errands, or make the beds,
I'm giving flowers to mother.

It's lots of fun pretending
And to hear my mother say,
"Thank you, dear, for all the flowers
You've given me today."

Clara Rader

GOD'S CREATION

God took the fragrance of a flower…
The majesty of a tree…
The gentleness of morning dew…
The calm of a quiet sea…
The beauty of the twilight hour…
The soul of a starry night…
The laughter of the rippling brook…
The grace of a bird in flight…
The tender care of an angel…
The faith of the mustard seed…
The patience of eternity…
The depth of a family's need…
Then God fashioned from these things
A creation like no other,
And when His masterpiece was through,
He called it simply — mother.

Herbert Farnham

IN ALL HONOR

Every man, for the sake of the great blessed Mother in Heaven,
and for the love of his own little mother on earth,
should handle all womankind gently,
and hold them in all honor.

Alfred, Lord Tennyson

A GRANDMOTHER'S PRAYER

Oh Lord, I do not ask for much,
Eternal beauty or youth or such:
Just give me a little hand to hold
And I'll forget that I'm growing old.
I do not ask for cloudless skies,
A life that's free from tears and sighs;
Just give me a little face to kiss
And anxious moments will turn to bliss.
For what is there, really, that means so much
As little hands that reach and touch,
As little eyes that search and see
Only the best in fragile me?
So let me grow more loving and wise
By looking at life through their wide eyes,
For through these little ones, Thou hast given
This grateful grandmother a glimpse of heaven.

Emily Ashley Tipton

THE PERFECT MOTHER

...Never was a woman more richly mother than this woman, bubbling over with a hundred little songs and scraps of gay nonsense to beguile a child from tears, and filled with wayward moods as she was; yet her hands were swift to tenderness and care and quiet brooding tending when need arose. Never was she more perfect mother than during the summers on the mountaintop when she could give herself freely to her children. She led them here and there in search of beauty, and she taught them to love cliffs and rugged rocks outlined against the sky, and to love also little dells where ferns and moss grow about a pool. Beauty she brought into her house, too, and filled the rooms with ferns and flowers.

Pearl S. Buck

IN EVERY HOME

Madonnas hallow every home;
O'er every roof where babies are
Shines high and pure a guiding star;
And mother hearts do always hear
Diviner music ringing clear.
And peace and love, good will on earth,
Are born with every baby's birth.

Author Unknown

18

MOTHER'S HANDS

Dear gentle hands have stroked my hair
　　And cooled my brow;
Soft hands that pressed me close
　　And seemed to know somehow
Those fleeting moods and erring thoughts
　　That cloud my day,
Which quickly melt beneath their suffrage
　　And pass away.

No other balm for earthly pain
　　Is half so sure,
No sweet caress so filled with love
　　Nor half so pure,
No other soul so close akin that understands,
　　No touch that brings such perfect peace
　　　　　as Mother's hands.

Author Unknown

Where we love is home.
　　Home is where our feet may leave
　　　　but not our hearts.

Oliver Wendell Holmes

for when you looked
        into my mother's eyes you knew,
            as if He had told you,
        why God sent her into the world —
            it was to open the minds
            of all who looked,
                    to beautiful thoughts.

James M. Barrie

HER LITTLE SHADOWS

I saw a young mother
With eyes full of laughter,
And two little shadows
Came following after.
Wherever she moved,
They were always right there —
Holding onto her skirts,
Hanging onto her chair,
Before her, behind her —
An adhesive pair.

"Don't you ever get weary
As, day after day,
Your two little tagalongs,
Get in your way?"

She smiled as she shook
Her pretty young head,
And I'll always remember
The words that she said:
"It's good to have shadows
That run when you run,
That laugh when you're happy
And hum when you hum —
For you only have shadows
When your life's filled with sun!"

Martha Wadsworth

THE MAGIC OF MOTHERS

There's magic in a mother's touch
And sunshine in her smile.
There's love in everything she does
To make our lives worthwhile.
We can find both hope and courage
Just by looking in her eyes;
Her laughter is a source of joy,
Her words are warm and wise.
There is kindness and compassion
To be found in her embrace,
And we see the light of heaven
Shining from a mother's face.

Reginald Holmes

 wise woman once said to me:
"There are only two lasting bequests
we can hope to give our children.
One of these is roots; the other, wings."

Hodding Carter

KITCHEN PRAYER

Lord of all pots and pans and things,
   Since I've not time to be
A saint by doing lovely things or
   Watching late with thee
Or dreaming in dawn's light or
   Storming heaven's gates,
Make me a saint by getting meals and
   Washing up the plates.

Although I must have Martha's hands,
   I have Mary's mind
And when I black the boots and shoes,
   Thy sandals, Lord, I find
I think of how they trod the earth,
   Each time I scrub the floor;
Accept this meditation, Lord,
   I haven't time for more.

Warm all the kitchen with Thy love
   And light it with Thy peace,
Forgive me all my worrying and make
   My grumbling cease.
Thou who didst love to give men food
   In room or by the sea,
Accept this service that I do,
   I do it unto Thee.

Author Unknown

The word "mother" has never been completely defined,
   for the earth is not acquainted
      with such divine words.

Charles Morgan

INVENTORY OF MOTHERS

Mothers have full cookie jars
For little girls to share,
Kisses for skinned noses, and
Her old high heels to wear.
Time to take you on her lap
To read a storybook,
Pretty aprons tied in bows
And applesauce to cook.
Scraps of cloth and bits of lace
To dress a dolly right,
Hands to tuck you safely in
At bedtime every night.

Doris Chalma Brock

YOUNG MOTHER

She holds him in her arms
   And murmurs lullabies;
While all the hope of
     motherhood
   Is shining in her eyes.

His eyes are pools that mirror
   Her dreams, her joys,
     her fears;
And in their depths are hidden
   The wonder of the years.

Kay Wissinger

Happiness makes its home in hearts furnished with love.

Hadin Marshall

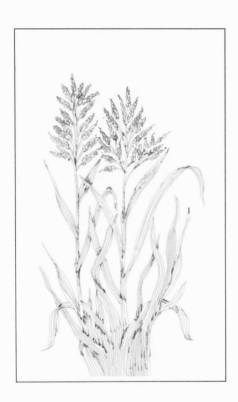

ONE-OF-A-KIND

Her warm words of praise,
    a kiss on the cheek,
The language of love
    that she knows how to speak —
These are the reasons
    a mother's unique.

Susan Bennett

EVERYDAY MADONNA

When Father carved our Christmas bird
And asked us each what we preferred,
As sure as summer follows spring
Came Mother's, "Please, I'll take a wing."

We children never wondered why
She did not sometimes take a thigh
Or choose a drumstick or a breast.
We thought she liked a wing the best.

She said it with such easy voice,
It seemed so certainly her choice....
I was a man before I knew
Why mothers do the things they do.

Richard Armour

There is no velvet so soft as mother's lap,
    no rose so lovely as her smile,
  no path so flowery
    as that imprinted with her footsteps.

Archbishop Thomson

My mother, who boasted of no degree,
  Was tutored in philosophy:
Five butter beans within a pod
  Were generosity from God;
A broom could sweep the shadows out;
  Churning put many a fear to rout;
A young pear tree in bridal veil
  Was beauty's triumph over the gale;
And every star that blinked on high
  Was proof that, body and breath put by,
No darkness was so vast, so deep,
  But that the Shepherd would find His sheep.

John Robert Quinn

WHAT IS A GRANDMOTHER?

A grandmother is someone whose warm, welcome smile
  Will always delight a child's heart,
She's someone who brightens all childhood affairs
  By playing a prominent part.
A grandmother's patience is never exhausted,
  She's gracious, thoughtful and kind,
She's a mixture of gentleness, warmth and affection,
  Of wisdom and humor combined.
A grandmother is someone who spends lots of time
  Telling stories of wonderful things,
With her goodness, her knowledge and understanding,
  What hours of pleasure she brings!
She's someone who fills all our lives with rich meaning
  And happiness year after year —
A grandmother is someone who's as sweet as can be
  Who just grows increasingly dear!

Katherine Nelson Davis

The most beautiful word in our language is Mother. Her tender hands wrought for us before we entered the world. Her weary feet never failed to carry her at night to see that we were safe in dreamland. In the long, dark hours she watched and prayed. She shared our sorrows and gave us our joys.

Author Unknown

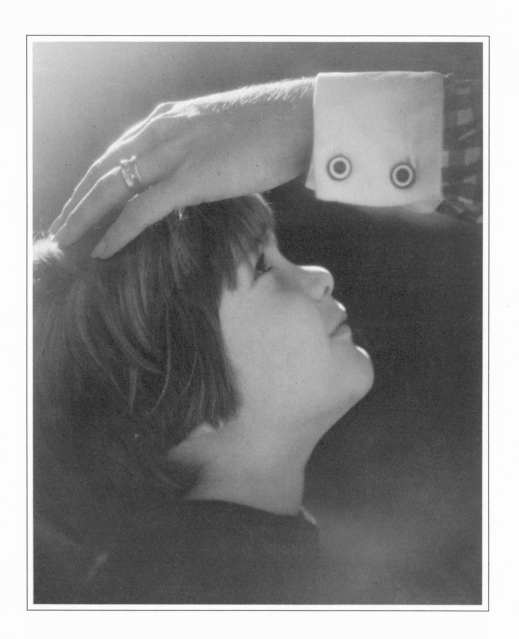

WHAT MOTHER IS TO ME

A song of hope, a fervent prayer;
A noble dream, and tender care;
A light of truth that makes me free —
All this my mother is to me.

A bank to put my worries in;
A balm to soothe my woes and sin;
A comforter where'er I be —
All this my mother is to me.

An eager heart my joys to share;
A valiant soul to bid me dare
The shining heights her eyes can see —
All this my mother is to me.

The one who loves with all her heart;
The one who always does her part
To help and guide so patiently —
All this my mother is to me.

An artist, poet, saint, or seer;
A fragrant flower, a memory dear —
My thoughts and words fail utterly
To tell what mother is to me.

J. Harold Gwynne

26

MOTHER'S LOVE

Her love is like an island
        In life's ocean, vast and wide,
A peaceful, quiet shelter
        From the wind, and rain, and tide.

Above it like a beacon light
        Shine faith, and truth, and prayer;
And through the changing scenes of life,
        I find a haven there.

Author Unknown

THE OLD ARM-CHAIR

I love it! I love it! and who shall dare
    To chide me for loving that old arm-chair?
    I've treasured it long as a sainted prize,
    I've bedew'd it with tears, and embalm'd it with sighs;
    'Tis bound by a thousand bands to my heart;
    Not a tie will break, not a link will start.
    Would ye learn the spell? — a mother sat there,
    And a sacred thing is that old arm-chair.

Eliza Cook

Mother in gladness, Mother in sorrow,
Mother today, and Mother tomorrow,
With arms ever open to enfold and caress you,
O Mother of Mine, may God keep you and bless you.

An Old English Prayer

MY MOTHER

Who fed me from her gentle breast,
And hushed me in her arms to rest,
And on my cheek sweet kisses pressed?
          My Mother.

When sleep forsook my open eye,
Who was it sang sweet lullaby,
And rocked me that I should not cry?
          My Mother.

Who sat and watched my infant head,
When sleeping on my cradle bed,
And tears of sweet affection shed?
          My Mother.

When pain and sickness made me cry,
Who gazed upon my heavy eye,
And wept for fear that I should die?
          My Mother.

Who dressed my doll in clothes so gay,
And taught me pretty how to play,
And minded all I had to say?
          My Mother.

Who ran to help me when I fell,
And would some pretty story tell,
Or kiss the place to make it well?
          My Mother.

28

Who taught my infant lips to pray,
And love God's holy book and day,
And walk in wisdom's pleasant way?
        My Mother.

And can I ever cease to be,
Affectionate and kind to thee,
Who was so very kind to me?
        My Mother.

Ah! no, the thought I cannot bear,
And if God please my life to spare,
I hope I shall reward thy care,
        My Mother.

When thou art feeble, old and gray,
My healthy arms shall be thy stay,
And I will soothe thy pains away,
        My Mother.

And when I see thee hang thy head,
'Twill be my turn to watch thy bed,
And tears of sweet affection shed,
        My Mother.

For God, who lives above the skies,
Would look with vengeance in His eyes,
If I should ever dare despise
        My Mother.

Jane Taylor

A GRANDMOTHER'S SPECIAL LOVE

What could be more precious
Than a grandmother's special love —
She always seems to know the things
That we are fondest of,
She's always ready with a smile
Or a loving word of praise,
Her laughter always brightens up
The cloudiest of days,
She has an understanding heart
That encourages and cheers,
The love she gives so freely
Grows deeper with the years,
Her wisdom and devotion
Are blessings from above —
Nothing could be more precious
Than a grandmother's special love.

Amanda Bradley

A MOTHER'S CREED

I believe in the eternal importance of the home
    as the fundamental institution of society.
I believe in the immeasurable possibilities
    of every boy and girl.
I believe in the imagination, the trust, the hopes
    and the ideals which dwell in the hearts
    of all children.
I believe in the beauty of nature, of art,
    of books, and of friendship.
I believe in the satisfactions of duty.
I believe in the little homely joys of everyday life.
I believe in the goodness of the great design
    which lies behind our complex world.
I believe in the safety and peace which surround
    us all through the overbrooding love of God.

Ozora Davis

DEFEAT

I know the puppy's very new,
And I know that he's lonely, too —
But puppy's place is in the shed,
And not with you, deep down in bed.
Tears will not move me — not at all,
Not even though he's soft and small,
And knows you when you come from play;
The shed's his place and there he'll stay, because —
Yes, he has lovely soft big paws,
And yes, I love his ears that flop....
Now, mind: not underneath! On top.

Barbara A. Jones

AN OLD-FASHIONED MOTHER

Blessed is the memory of an old-fashioned mother.
It floats to us now like the beautiful perfume of some woodland blossoms.
The music of our voices may be lost, but the entrancing melody
of hers will echo in our soul forever.
Other faces will fade away and be forgotten, but hers will shine
on until the light from heaven's portal
will glorify our own.

Author Unknown

PARADOX

My son is quiet —
He loves to plant flowers,
He'll listen to records
In the playroom for hours.
    My daughter's a riot!
    She never sits still —
    She handles a football
    With daring and skill!
My son is mild
In temper and tone,
And his books are the key
To a world of his own.
    My daughter is wild
    And impressively loud —
    Already the leader
    Of the neighborhood crowd.
It didn't turn out
As I figured it would,
But I wouldn't change them.
(Not that I could!)
I'll fan my small Shakespeare's
Literary spark
And grab hasty kisses
From my young Joan of Arc!

Mary Dawson Hughes

NOBODY KNOWS — BUT MOTHER

Nobody knows of the work it makes
    To keep the home together,
Nobody knows of the steps it takes,
    Nobody knows — but mother.

Nobody listens to childish woes,
    Which kisses only smother;
Nobody's pained by naughty blows,
    Nobody knows — only mother.

Nobody knows of the sleepless care
    Bestowed on baby brother;
Nobody knows of the tender prayer,
    Nobody — only mother.

Nobody knows of the lessons taught
    Of loving one another;
Nobody knows of the patience sought,
    Nobody — only mother.

Nobody knows of the anxious fears,
    Lest darlings may not weather
The storm of life in after years,
    Nobody knows — but mother.

Nobody kneels at the throne above
    To thank the Heavenly Father
For that sweetest gift — a mother's love;
    Nobody can — but mother.

The Fireside

A mother's heart, so like His own it is!
    True motherhood has touched His garment's hem
For strength and wisdom, and I am quite sure
    We honor Him the day we honor them.

Grace Noll Crowell

WHEN AMY HELPS ME COOK

We use every burner on the stove
And every bowl and pan I own—
We let imaginations roam
When Amy helps me cook.
When we make cookies or cake or pie,
We always exhaust the flour supply—
We wear the most part, she and I,
When Amy helps me cook.
Of course, it takes me twice as long,
And things have a way of going wrong,
But my kitchen's filled with happy song
When Amy helps me cook.
Her daddy is free with the compliments;
He'll even eat our "accidents,"
For Love is the main ingredient
When Amy helps me cook.

Margaret Lindsey

She was always there
and would always wear
a smiling face;
she gave advice,
a helping hand,
a warm embrace—
my mother.

Kay Andrew

THE LOVE OF A MOTHER

There is an enduring tenderness in the love of a mother to a son that transcends all other affections of the heart. It is neither to be chilled by selfishness, nor daunted by danger, nor weakened by worthlessness, nor stifled by ingratitude. She will sacrifice every comfort to his convenience; she will surrender every pleasure to his enjoyment; she will glory in his fame and exalt in his prosperity; and if adversity overtake him, he will be the dearer to her by misfortune; and if disgrace settle upon his name, she will still love and cherish him; and if all the world beside cast him off, she will be all the world to him.

Washington Irving

A MOTHER

When God looked down upon the earth
And chose to put new blessings there,
    Gifts from above
    To show His love,
And lighten earthly joy and care,
He gave the sky the sunset glow;
Gave fragrance to the lily's blow;
    Gave laughter gay
    To children's play,
And then to every yearning soul
He gave that gift of tenderest worth —
A Mother.

The lily's sweetness is forgotten,
And sunset splendors fade to gray;
    But fresh and dear,
    Through changing year,
Through quiet night, or eager day,
The love of her we love the best
Lives closely shrined within each breast.
    Bless Heaven for —
    A Mother.

Sarah N. Latham

MOTHER

I think it was a girlish hand,
  Unlined, well tended, when it held
At first, my clinging baby hand
  In gentle grasp by love impelled.

I think it was a youthful face
  That bent above me as I lay
Asleep, and bright the eyes that watched
  My rest in that forgotten day.

I think it was a slender form
  That bore my weight on tiring arm,
And swift young feet that watched my steps
  To guide them from the ways of harm.

But years and cares have changed that form
  And face and hand; have streaked with gray
The hair; yet is the heart as full
  Of love as in that other day.

And she has her reward, not fame,
  Or baubles bought in any mart,
But motherhood's brave crown, the love
  And homage of her own child's heart.

Clara Aiken Speer

AN ANGEL ON EARTH

My mother was an angel upon earth. She was a minister of blessing to all human beings within her sphere of action. Her heart was the abode of heavenly purity. She had no feelings but of kindness and beneficence, yet her mind was as firm as her temper was mild and gentle. She had known sorrow, but her sorrow was silent. Had she lived to the age of the Patriarchs, every day of her life would have been filled with clouds of goodness and of love. She had been fifty years the delight of my father's heart. If there is existence and retribution beyond the grave, my mother is happy. But if virtue alone is happiness below, never was existence upon earth more blessed than hers.

John Quincy Adams

ONLY A MOTHER

There are times when only a mother's heart
    Can share the joy we feel
    When something that we've dreamed about
    Quite suddenly is real!
    There are times when only a mother's love
    Can understand our tears,
    Our bitter disappointments
    And all our childish fears.
    There are times when only a mother's words
    Can make us want to smile

And give us the assurance
That makes life more worthwhile.
There are times when only a mother's faith
Can help us on life's way
And inspire in us the confidence
We need from day to day.
Yes, so often through our lifetime,
Whether skies are gray or blue,
It seems that there are countless times
When only a mother will do.

Mary Dawson Hughes

GOD TO A MOTHER

Do not fear
To nod your head a bit.
Lean back and sit
Comfortably, here against the pew.
You had so many things to do
About the house
Before you came:
There was the baby's bath,
There was the game
Of dominoes you straightened out
For Dick and Bill.
Your hands are still
Trembling from rushing so
Before the time for you to go.
Relax and rest a bit
Now, as you sit
Before my sanctuary.
You are so very tired.
What if you miss a word or two?
It is no sin. Oh have no fear!
It is enough that you are here.

Myrtle Vorst Sheppard

WOMAN DEEPLY LOVED

To see and watch her is to know
That she is deeply loved. Her face
Reflects this. Love has left its trace
In her serenity, the glow
Of deep contentment in her eyes,
Her joyous laugh, the cheerful way
She goes about her work each day.
Love haloes women, beautifies
The plainest face, for more than bread
To every woman is the knowing
She is cherished; keeps her glowing
With confidence, affection-fed:
Her happiness, so much a part
Of love, enshrined within her heart.

Velma West Sykes

Though distance may come between a mother and her child,
the bond that holds them close will never weaken —
the love they share will never be more than a memory apart.

Dean Walley

38

LOVE NEAREST TO HEAVEN

A mother's love! What can compare with it! Of all things on earth, it comes nearest to divine love in heaven.

A mother's love means a life's devotion — and sometimes a life's sacrifice — with but one thought, one hope and one feeling; that her children will grow up healthy and strong, free from evil habits and able to provide for themselves. Her sole wish is that they may do their part like men and women, avoid dangers and pitfalls, and when dark hours come, trust in Providence to give them strength, patience and courage to bear up bravely.

Happy is the mother when her heart's wish is answered, and happy are her sons and daughters when they can feel that they have contributed to her noble purpose, and, in some measure, repaid her unceasing, unwavering love and devotion.

Author Unknown

THE WAY OF A MOTHER

Somehow she never seems to see
The change that the years have made in me,
Her hands have the soft and gentle touch
That I, as a small child, loved so much.

Her voice, in the same familiar way,
Soothes the hurts of a too-harsh day;
And her patient love and tender care
Follow my footsteps like a prayer.

Thank God that mothers are so blind
To the babyhood we leave behind,
For often in life, with its care and pain,
It is sweet to be thought a child again.

Katherine Edelman

Whatever is good and true in my thoughts,
Whatever is beautiful and joyful in my spirit,
Whatever is courageous in my actions,
Whatever is faithful and understanding in my heart —
Are gifts from my wonderful mother.

Barbara Kunz Loots

HOME

Home is the sound of happy voices;
Home is cookies in the oven,
A little bit of scoldin'
And a great big heap of lovin' —
Home is a cheery fire,
A door that's always open —
Someone to share your secret dreams
And hope the things you're hopin';
Home is windows always lighted
And the warmth of love inside,
A little bit of heaven
Where peace and joy reside!

Rita Davis

Blessed be the hand
    that prepares a pleasure for a child,
      for there is no saying
        when and where it may bloom forth.

Douglas Jerrold

DEAREST MOTHER

There's something about a mother
That makes her mean so much —
There's a gentle softness in her voice,
A magic in her touch —
There's something about a mother
That makes her seem so wise —
A special comfort in her smile
And loveshine in her eyes.
There's something about a mother
That makes her somehow know
How to take a hurt away
And how to make love grow.
There's something about a mother
That makes her hear each call —
And there's something about my mother
That makes her the dearest of all.

Karen Ravn

As soft and gentle
    as candlelight —
Ever welcoming,
    ever bright —
      this is a mother's love.

Amy Cassity

The family
  is like a garden,
  with joy
    for all to share,
With tender, growing blossoms
  that thrive on love
    and care,
And when
  the flowers are gathered
For a very special day,
They make
  a bright and beautiful
    happiness bouquet.

Mary Alice Loberg

A PARTNERSHIP WITH GOD

A partnership with God is motherhood;
What strength, what purity, what self-control,
What love, what wisdom should belong to her
Who helps God fashion an immortal soul.

Author Unknown

FOREVER SPRING

The seasons come
And the seasons go
And many the changes they bring;
But in the warmth
Of a mother's heart
It is forever spring.

Amy Cassity

Men are what their mothers make them.

Ralph Waldo Emerson

...The angels, whispering to one another,
Can find, among their burning terms of love,
None so devotional as that of "Mother"....

Edgar Allan Poe

Every mother has the breathtaking privilege of sharing with God in the creation of new life. She helps bring into existence a soul that will endure for all eternity.

Every mother also has the unique honor of nurturing and developing the bit of divine greatness in her child. Through her loving and devoted care, this youthful power can be directed from its earliest years to work for the glory of God and the benefit of others and thus contribute to its own temporal and eternal advantage.

Yes, a good mother can reach beyond the sanctuary of her home and help renew the face of the earth.

James Keller

MY MOTHER'S EYES

O wondrous eyes...
Filled with tremendous silence!
They shine
Wide with vision,
Level with courage,
Dark with challenge,
Deep with defense,
Mighty with magic,
Mute with mystery,
Tender with tears,
Serene with peace,
Lighted with faith,
Winged with hope,
Immortal with love.

Meredith Gray

The real religion of the world comes from women
much more than from men —
from mothers most of all, who carry the key
of our souls in their bosoms.

Oliver Wendell Holmes

DEAR MOTHER

Dear Mother, when I think of you
   I think of all things good and true,
Of trees and lanes and babbling brooks,
   Of mountains, hills and shady nooks.

I think of flowers of every hue,
   Of roses kissed by morning dew,
Of violets blue and daisies bright,
   And stately lilies, pure and white.

I think of cloudless skies of blue,
   And, Mother dear, because of you,
I think of robins in the spring
   And of the joyous songs they sing.

I think of fields of golden grain,
   And of the soft refreshing rain.
I think of honeybees in clover
   And of God's sunshine bubbling over.

I think of children's happy faces,
   Of grand old ladies in their laces,
Of all men, noble, brave and true,
   Because of Mothers just like you.

Pauline Mengedoth

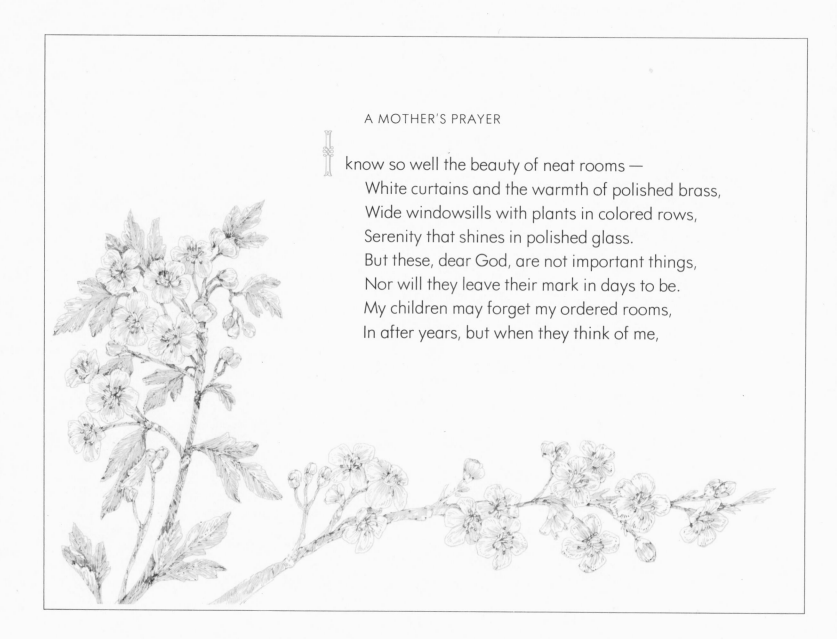

A MOTHER'S PRAYER

I know so well the beauty of neat rooms —
  White curtains and the warmth of polished brass,
  Wide windowsills with plants in colored rows,
  Serenity that shines in polished glass.
  But these, dear God, are not important things,
  Nor will they leave their mark in days to be.
  My children may forget my ordered rooms,
  In after years, but when they think of me,

May they remember I laughed much, dear God,
And heard their dreams and shared their gaiety.
And that I read them stories from old books
Of brave, fair days, and sometimes made them see
A wider world — beyond our sturdy walls.
Make them remember that I deemed it more
My task to be as gentle as I could
Than keep clean rugs upon a dusted floor.

Helen Welshimer

A HOME FILLED WITH LOVE

Give me no treasures,
    no silver or gold,
    give me true hearts
    and warm hands to hold.
Give me no mansions,
    no countries to roam,
    give me a family
    where love is at home.

Mary Alice Loberg

46

BLESS THESE HANDS

Help me, dear Lord, as a mother, I pray,
And bless these hands folded in prayer today.
May they be ever strong as they guide, as they teach,
Being never too far for a child to reach.
May they never, with selfishness, try to dissuade,
Nor too quickly punish, nor too slowly aid.
May they point out the pleasures in laughter and song,
And may they show, wisely, the right from the wrong,
So that one day I'll know that I've helped all I can
To make her a woman, to make him a man.

Alice Walley

WHY GOD MADE MOTHERS

God knew that everybody needs
Someone to show the way,
He knew that babies need someone
To care for them each day.
He knew they needed someone sweet
To soothe their baby cries,
To teach them how to walk and talk,
And sing them lullabies.
That's why God made mothers.

He knew small children need someone
To lend a guiding hand,
To answer all their questions,
And to smile and understand,
Someone to read them storybooks,
To teach them wrong from right,
To show them wonderful new games,
And hear their prayers at night.
That's why God made mothers.

And then throughout their childhood years,
God knew that children need
Someone to smile at them with pride,
Encourage each new deed.
As they grow up and all their lives,
God knew that everywhere
All children need a mother's heart
To understand and care,
And that's why God made mothers.

Katherine Nelson Davis

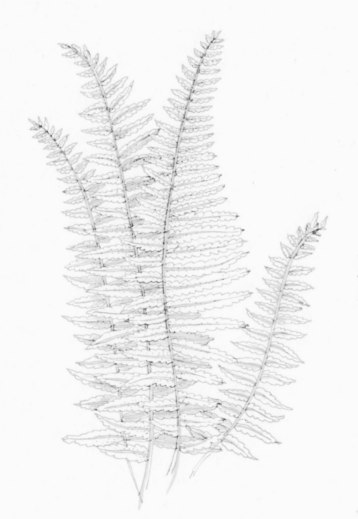

THE MOTHER IN THE HOUSE

For such as you, I do believe,
Spirits their softest carpets weave
And spread them out with gracious hand
Wherever you walk, wherever you stand.

For such as you, of scent and dew,
Spirits their rarest nectar brew,
And where you sit and where you sup,
Pour beauty's elixir in your cup.

For all day long, like other folk,
You bear the burden, wear the yoke,
And yet when I look in your eyes at eve,
You are lovelier than ever, I do believe.

Hermann Hagedorn

No joy in nature is so sublimely affecting as the joy of a mother
at the good fortune of her child.

Jean Paul Friedrich Richter

The family is one of nature's masterpieces.

George Santayana

48

MY TRUST

A picture memory brings to me:
   I look across the years and see
   Myself beside my mother's knee.

I feel her gentle hand restrain
My selfish moods, and know again
A child's blind sense of wrong and pain.

But wiser now, a man gray grown,
My childhood's needs are better known,
My mother's chastening love I own.

John Greenleaf Whittier

Mother is the name for God in the lips and hearts of little children.

William Makepeace Thackeray

She walks in elegance whose heart
Is filled with beauty, like the spring.
   Her gentleness is but a part
Of all the joy her graces bring.

Charlotte Carpenter

I LOVE YOU

A mother says "I love you"
   in so many ways:
   with crisp, clean sheets
   and warm mittens on winter mornings,
   with decorated birthday cakes
   and Christmas cookies,
   and eggs cooked
   just the way you like them.
A mother says "I love you"
   when she leaves the porchlight on for you
   and picks up your clothes,
   when she keeps your secrets,
   feeds your pets
   and tapes your homemade Valentines
   to the refrigerator door.
But most of all,
   a mother says "I love you"
   by filling a home
   with warmth,
   tenderness
   and love.

Mary Ellen Lowe

A MOTHER'S BIRTHDAY

Lord Jesus, Thou hast known
    A mother's love and tender care;
        And Thou wilt hear
        While for my own
    Mother most dear
I make this birthday prayer.

Protect her life, I pray,
    Who gave the gift of life to me;
        And may she know,
        From day to day,
    The deepening glow
Of joy that comes from Thee.

As once upon her breast
    Fearless and well content I lay,
        So let her heart,
        On Thee at rest,
    Feel fear depart
And trouble fade away.

Ah, hold her by the hand,
    As once her hand held mine;
        And though she may
        Not understand
    Life's winding way,
Lead her in peace divine.

I cannot pay my debt
    For all the love that she has given;
        But Thou, love's Lord,
        Wilt not forget
    Her due reward —
Bless her in earth and heaven.

Henry van Dyke

BECAUSE SHE IS A MOTHER

She broke the bread into two fragments,
    and gave them to the children, who ate with avidity.
    "She hath kept none for herself," grumbled the Sergeant.
    "Because she is not hungry," said a soldier.
    "Because she is a mother," said the Sergeant.

Victor Hugo

50

STUDY IN CONTRAST

"Isn't it discouraging,"
She asked, "to work all day
At all your drudging household tasks
With never any pay?"
My friend then spoke of contrasts
(For she had a career),
Of office gossip and intrigue —
I listened with one ear.
The other one, I must admit,
Heard echoes of the day
When birthday party laughter
Rang throughout the house — no pay?
Oh, true it is, my overtime
Is not repaid by check,
But I have felt a baby's arms
Curl warmly round my neck.
My typing now is somewhat less
Than eighty words a minute,
But I have ironed a fresh white shirt
And loved the husband in it.
I smiled at her, my working friend,
And as we rose to part,
She had wages in her purse,
But I held riches in my heart.

Doris Chalma Brock

MOTHER LOVE

What is mother love?
    the flame
  that kindles tribute
    to her name…
  that lights our path
    and guides our aim…
  this is mother love.
What is mother love?
    the flower
  whose fragrance sweetens
    every hour…
  that never fades through
    sun or shower…
  this is mother love.
What is mother love?
    the smile
  that lifts our thoughts
    to things worthwhile…
  that warms and brightens
    every mile…
  that is mother love.

Margaret Benton

LIKE A MOTHER'S VOICE

We were talking of bells
  And one used one simile
  And one another
  To describe their sweet tones,
  Then,
  One who had not learned
  Hackneyed phrases in a school
  But had known a loving mother's guidance
  Said,
"I know of some bells
  In the little town of B —
  And they are the sweetest sounding
  Of any I have heard.
  They sound like" —
  Here words failed him for a moment —
  Then,
"They sound like
  A mother's voice calling."

And I wonder if in all the world
  One could, indeed, find sweeter sound
  Than a mother's voice calling,
  Calling a beloved child.

Homer C. Fisher

When God thought of mother,
    He must have laughed with satisfaction
    and framed it quickly —
        so rich, so deep, so divine,
            so full of soul, power and beauty
            was the conception.

Henry Ward Beecher

MOTHER LOVE

MOTHERHOOD

Womanliness means only motherhood;
     All love begins and ends there, — roams enough,
     But, having run the circle, rests at home.

Robert Browning

All the love we come to know in life
     springs from the love we knew as children.

James Langdon

The many make the household,
But only one the home.

James Russell Lowell

The mother's heart is the child's schoolroom.

Henry Ward Beecher

MOTHERS ARE WONDERFUL

Mothers should know everything,
   like just how high is up,
   how to kiss away a hurt
   or how to wash a pup!
Mothers should know everything,
   like how to mend old toys
   and how to tell a story
   that delights small girls and boys.
Mothers should know everything,
   like how to fly a kite,
   what makes a lovely flower bloom,
   why stars come out at night.
Mothers should know everything,
   even why the sky is blue!
Yes, mothers should know everything,
   and the wonder is,
       they do!

Katherine Plumb

A mother has, perhaps,
   the hardest earthly lot.
Yet no mother
   worthy of the name
   ever gave herself thoroughly
   for her child
   who did not feel that,
   after all,
   she reaped what
   she had sown.

Henry Ward Beecher

A MOTHER'S PRAYER

Father in Heaven, make me wise,
   So that my gaze may never meet
A question in my children's eyes;
   God keep me always kind and sweet,

And patient, too, before their need;
   Let each vexation know its place,
Let gentleness be all my creed,
   Let laughter live upon my face!

A mother's day is very long,
   There are so many things to do!
But never let me lose my song
   Before the hardest day is through.

Margaret E. Sangster

THE PICTURE

The painter has with his brush transferred the landscape
         to the canvas with such fidelity that the trees and grasses
      seem almost real; he has made even the face of a maiden
         seem instinct with life, but there is one picture
      so beautiful that no painter has ever been able perfectly
            to reproduce it, and that is the picture of the mother
                  holding in her arms her babe.

William Jennings Bryan

A MOTHER UNDERSTANDS

When mother sits beside my bed
    At night, and strokes and smooths my head,
    And kisses me, I think, some way,
    How naughty I have been all day;
    Of how I waded in the brook,
    And of the cookies that I took,
    And how I smashed a window light
    A-rassling — me and Bobby White —
    And tore my pants, and told a lie;
    It almost makes me want to cry
    When mother pats and kisses me;
    I'm just as sorry as can be,
    But I don't tell her so — no, sir.
    She knows it all; you can't fool her.

Author Unknown

A MOTHER'S HEART

The door that leads to a mother's heart
    Is always open wide,
    And in her heart is a special place
    Where peace and love abide.
    There is no lock on a mother's heart,
    Her children freely go
    For a pat on the cheek or a comforting word
    Or something they want to know.
    Through years of work and prayer she's learned
    Her wise and tender art,
    For the nearest thing to the love of God
    Is the love of a mother's heart.

Barbara Burrow

TRANSFORMATION

Mighty is the force of motherhood! It transforms all things by its vital heat; it turns timidity into fierce courage, and dreadless defiance into tremulous submission; it turns thoughtlessness into foresight, and yet stills all anxiety into calm content; it makes selfishness become self-denial, and gives even to hard vanity the glance of admiring love.

George Eliot

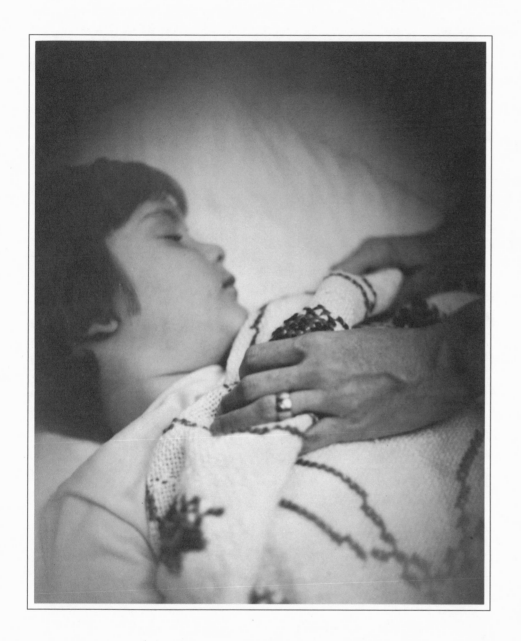

MEMORIES AND MOTHER

When Mother came to our room
To tuck us in at night,
Her face would look so gentle
In the soft, bedside light.

And though we may not always
Have behaved our best that day,
She'd let us know she loved us
In a very special way:
An extra fold to the coverlet,
A little pat, a hug,
And we'd settle down to dreamland,
Feeling safe and snug.

And of all the childhood memories
That there have ever been,
We love best to recall the times
When Mother tucked us in.

Mary Rita Hurley

Into the woman's keeping is committed the destiny of the generations to come after us. In bringing up your children, you mothers must remember that while it is essential to be loving and tender, it is no less essential to be wise and firm. Foolishness and affection must not be treated as interchangeable terms; and besides training your sons and daughters in the softer and milder virtues, you must seek to give them those stern and hardy qualities which in after life they will surely need.

Some children will go wrong in spite of the best training; and some will go right even when their surroundings are most unfortunate.... Teach boys and girls alike that they are not to look forward to lives spent in avoiding difficulties; teach them that work, for themselves and also for others, is not a curse but a blessing; seek to make them happy, to make them enjoy life, but seek also to make them face life with steadfast resolution, and to do their whole duty before God and to man. Surely, she who can thus train her sons and daughters is thrice fortunate among women.

Theodore Roosevelt

A mother always knows what you need...
sometimes that's all you need to know.

Karen Ravn

Beautiful, the earth around her —
peaceful, the sky above,
Harmony and joy surround her —
gentle is a mother's love.

Edward Cunningham

THE PRINCESS

I loved her, one
Not learned, save in gracious household ways,
Nor perfect, nay, but full of tender wants,
No Angel, but a dearer being, all dipt
In Angel instincts, breathing Paradise,
Interpreter between the gods and men,
Who look'd all native to her place, and yet
On tiptoe seem'd to touch upon a sphere
Too gross to tread,
   and all male minds perforce
Sway'd to her from their orbits
   as they moved,
And girdled her with music. Happy he
With such a mother! Faith in womenkind
Beats with his blood,
   and trust in all things high
Comes easy to him, and tho' he trip and fall,
He shall not blind his soul with clay.

Alfred, Lord Tennyson

Mother is the heart of a home.

Steven Rustad

MOTHER

The noblest thoughts my soul can claim,
   The holiest words my tongue can frame,
Unworthy are to praise the name
   More sacred than all other.
An infant, when her love first came —
A man, I find it just the same;
Reverently I breathe her name,
   The blessed name of mother.

George Griffith Fetter

A woman who runs her house well is both its queen and its subject. She is the one who makes work possible for her husband and children; she protects them from worries, feeds them and cares for them. She is Minister of Finance, and, thanks to her, the household budget is balanced. She is Minister of Fine Arts, and it is to her doing if the house or apartment has charm. She is Minister of Family Education and responsible for the boys' entry into school and college and the girls' cleverness and cultivation. A woman should be proud of her success in making her house into a perfect little world as the greatest statesman of his in organizing a nation's affairs.

André Maurois

WHAT IS A MOTHER?

A mother is someone to shelter and guide us,
To love us, whatever we do,
With a warm understanding and infinite patience
And wonderful gentleness, too.
How often a mother means swift reassurance
In soothing our small, childish fears,
How tenderly mothers watch over their children
And treasure them all through the years!
The heart of a mother is full of forgiveness
For any mistake, big or small,

And generous always in helping her family,
Whose needs she has placed above all.
A mother can utter a word of compassion
And make all our cares fall away,
She can brighten a home with the sound of her laughter
And make life delightful and gay.
A mother possesses incredible wisdom
And wonderful insight and skill—
In each human heart is that one special corner
Which only a mother can fill!

Katherine Nelson Davis

A mother laughs our laughter,
Sheds our tears,
Returns our love,
Fears our fears.
She lives our joys,
Cares our cares
And all our hopes and dreams
    she shares.

Dean Walley

A MOTHER'S PICTURE

"A lady, the loveliest ever the sun looked down upon,
You must paint for me.
O, if I could only make you see
The clear blue eyes, the tender smile,
The sovereign sweetness, the gentle grace,
The woman's soul and the angel's face,
That are beaming on me all the while,
But I need not speak these foolish words;
One word tells you all I would say,
She is my mother: and you will agree
That all the rest may be thrown away."

Alice Cary

Strength and dignity are her clothing,
    and she laughs at the time to come.
She opens her mouth with wisdom,
    and the teaching of kindness is on her tongue.
She looks well to the ways of her household,
    and does not eat the bread of idleness.
Her children rise up and call her blessed....

Proverbs 31:25-28

Mothers have a way of making the difficult times easier
                    and the good times truly wonderful.

James Langdon

There is no spectacle on earth more appealing
        than that of a beautiful woman
            in the act of cooking dinner for someone she loves.

Thomas Wolfe

The instruction received at the mother's knee,
　　and the paternal lessons,
　　　together with the pious and sweet souvenirs of the fireside
　　　　are never effaced entirely from the soul.

Lamennais

A MOTHER'S LOVE

You see a mother's love
　　in a table set with care,
　a stack of mending
　　　by her favorite chair,
　a room that's decorated
　　　with her own special flair —
These are the things love is made of.

You see it when she cooks
　　her family's favorite dishes,
　listens to each problem,
　　　the secret dreams and wishes,
　when she tucks the children in
　　　with loving hugs and kisses —
These are the things love is made of.

Barbara Burrow

Mothers...
　Think of the shoes they tied for us,
　The clothes they washed and dried for us,
　The butter and jelly they spread for us,
　The times they made the bed for us;
　Think of the joys they brought to us
　And the lessons of love they taught to us!

Louis Conrad Hill

Youth fades;
　　love droops;
　　the leaves of
　　friendship fall:
A mother's
　　secret hope outlives
　　them all.

Oliver Wendell Holmes

Nothing speaks so loudly, or is heard so plainly,
　　　　as the silent voice of a mother's love.

Emily Ashley Tipton

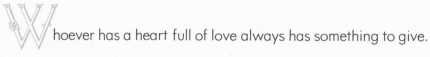

Whoever has a heart full of love always has something to give.

Pope John XXIII

Love is found
    in a quiet place,
    in soft, sweet words…
    in a mother's face.

Karen Middaugh

CORSAGE

Mother, Mother,
The florist's boy knocks,
With his hat in his hand
And a great green box.

Hurry, lift the cover;
See, untie the bow…
Four pink camellias
Fastened in a row.

Mother, Mother,
Please, and shut your eyes!
This is from me.
This is a surprise.

Yellow dandelions
With tangly silk hair…
Mother, Mother,
Which shall you wear?

Ethel Jacobson

RECOGNITION

"I don't want to hear another word!"
    I hear my daughter scold.
"Dear me!" I think, "She's awfully strict
    For a playful three-year-old!"
She rolls her big eyes heavenward
    And sighs with great disdain.
"What am I going to do with you?!"
    Her dolls hear her complain.
"Sit down! Be still! Hold out your hands!
    Do you have to walk so slow?
Pick up your toys! Go brush your teeth!
    Eat all your carrots! Blow!"
I start to tell her how gentle
    A mother ought to be,
When blushingly I realize
    She's imitating ME!

Rebecca Shaw

MOTHER'S BOYS

Yes, I know there are stains on my carpet,
　　The traces of small muddy boots;
And I see your fair tapestry glowing,
　　All spotless with flowers and fruits.

And I know that my walls are disfigured
　　With prints of small fingers and hands;
And that your own household most truly
　　In immaculate purity stands.

And I know that my parlor is littered
　　With many odd treasures and toys,
While your own is in daintiest order,
　　Unharmed by the presence of boys.

And I know that my room is invaded
　　Quite boldly all hours of the day,
While you sit in yours unmolested
　　And dream the soft quiet away.

Yes, I know there are four little bedsides
　　Where I must stand watchful each night,
While you may go out in your carriage
　　And flash in your dresses so bright.

Now, I think I'm a neat little woman,
　　And I like my house orderly, too;
And I'm fond of all dainty belongings,
　　Yet I would not change places with you.

No! keep your fair home with its order,
　　Its freedom from bother and noise;
And keep your own fanciful leisure,
　　But give me my four splendid boys.

Author Unknown

66

GOD CREATED LOVE

God created everything:
The golden daffodils,
The serenade of birds that sing,
The green and rolling hills.
He made the rainbow in the sky,
The meadows and the lanes.
He made each lovely butterfly,
The mountains and the plains.
He made the summer breeze so mild,
The moon and stars above,
But when He created Mother —
Then God created love.

Raymond Mathews

Thousands of stars in the evening sky,
Thousands of shells on the shore together,
Thousands of birds that go winging by,
Thousands of flowers in the sunny weather.

Thousands of dewdrops to greet the dawn,
Thousands of bees in the fields of clover,
Thousands of butterflies dot the lawn,
But only one mother the wide world over.

Margaret Lindsey

Set in Futura Light, a typeface designed by Paul Renner
and introduced in 1927.
The paper is Hallmark Ivory Vellux.
Designed by Myron McVay.